BO

M

BO SCHEMBECHLER
1929-2006

"THERE WAS A TIME AROUND HERE WHEN THEY CHANTED, 'BO IS GOD! BO IS GOD!' HE WASN'T OF COURSE, BUT NOW THAT HE'S GONE, EVERYWHERE YOU TURN YOU HEAR THEIR NAMES IN THE SAME SENTENCE. HE WILL BE MISSED. GOD, HOW BO WILL BE MISSED."

—MITCH ALBOM, AUTHOR OF

BO SCHEMBECHLER'S AUTOBIOGRAPHY

ISBN 10: 1-59670-255-9
ISBN 13: 978-1-59670-255-4

© Sports Publishing L.L.C.

Front cover and title page photo by Tony Tomsic/Sports Illustrated
Back cover photo by AP/WWP

SportsPublishingLLC.com

Publishers: Peter L. Bannon and Joseph J. Bannon Sr.
Senior managing editor: Susan M. Moyer
Developmental editor: Doug Hoepker
Art director and cover design: K. Jeffrey Higgerson
Photo editor: Erin Linden-Levy
Graphic design: Dustin Hubbart

Sports Publishing L.L.C.
804 North Neil Street
Champaign, IL 61820
Phone: 1-877-424-2665
Fax: 217-363-2073
SportsPublishingLLC.com

Printed in the United States of America.

FOREWORD

BY JACK EBLING

ON THURSDAY, NOVEMBER 16, 2006, a Man's Man was supposed to meet with his doctor.

At age 77, after *two* quadruple-bypass surgeries, it seemed like a wise thing to do.

But Glenn Edward "Bo" Schembechler had a more important meeting in mind.

When one of his protégés, Michigan head football coach Lloyd Carr, asked Schembechler to speak to the Wolverines the night before they left for Columbus and a head-on collision with the Ohio State Buckeyes, nothing else mattered.

If God needed a stubborn German in heaven, he'd just have to wait a little longer. Michigan had a game to win. And a guy who won 194 of them with the Maize and Blue from 1969-89 had one more message in him.

Not "The Team, The Team, The Team." And not "Those Who Stay Will Be Champions," as important as those mantras had been to the Wolverines.

The final address to the troops from "Gen. George Patton Schembechler" dealt primarily with Wolverine Pride. No one exemplified that better than the speaker himself, a person of undying principle and unwavering loyalty.

He came to Michigan from Miami, Ohio, where he kept his "M" and merely switched colors from red to blue. Schembechler's passion? It made the trip, too.

But not before the Barberton, Ohio, native and fireman's son played tackle for Woody Hayes' Redskins and pitched a little baseball for Miami. It wasn't the last time Hayes would bark orders. Eventually, the pup would bark back.

Schembechler's coaching career began with one-year stops at Presbyterian and Bowling Green. When he joined Ara Parseghian and a star-studded staff at Northwestern, no one ever imagined the Wildcats would be winless in 1957.

None of that mattered to Hayes, who hired Schembechler away from Parseghian in an all-Miami transaction. "The Cradle of Coaches" would soon rock the world.

Bo Schembechler is lifted to his team's shoulders during the celebration following Michigan's defeat of Nebraska, 27-23, in the 1986 Fiesta Bowl. *AP/WWP*

On the banks of the Olentangy River, Hayes threw OSU chairs at his trusted aide. Schembechler learned to throw them back.

Together, they took the Buckeyes to a Big Ten title, an unbeaten season and a runner-up finish in both polls in 1961. Any chance at a national championship ended when The Ohio State University's faculty rejected a Rose Bowl invitation.

The last game of '61 spoke volumes about a unique relationship. In tight games, with Schembechler calling plays from the press box, Hayes would hang on his offensive coordinator's every word. When OSU beat Michigan 50-20, Hayes was hard of hearing.

"He'd always say, 'Don't leave me, Bo!'" Schembechler remembered with a laugh. "That day, as soon as we started blowing them out, I couldn't even get him on the phone. For more than a quarter, I had no contact at all. Everyone said I called the two-point play to go for 50. Hey, that wasn't me!"

When Schembechler returned to Miami a year later for his first head coaching assignment, no one could have imagined what would happen six successful years later. Destiny, in the Wolverines' eyes. The unthinkable, if you lived in Columbus.

Michigan had just completed its most successful season since 1964, the only year with a Rose Bowl bid under mild-mannered Bump Elliott. But when a 50-20 loss in Ohio Stadium left Michigan home for the holidays at 8-2, it was time for a change.

It didn't help the mood in Ann Arbor that the sophomore-laden Buckeyes rolled to a national title by beating USC and O.J. Simpson in Pasadena. The challenge for new athletic director Don Canham was to find a Woody of his own.

Canham, a marketing whiz and arguably the greatest athletic administrator in NCAA history, began his search with one essential bit of knowledge—that he didn't know enough to do it alone.

The first person to mention Schembechler's name was legendary "MEEE-chigan" broadcaster Bob Ufer. Bob Shaw, an Elliott aide who recruited Ohio, also gave a recommendation.

But when Canham called another Michigan man, Los Angeles Rams head coach George Allen, Schembechler's name was the second one mentioned. And when Canham and Elliott met Jets owner Sonny Werblin in New York, there was that name again!

"He told me I ought to talk to Joe Paterno at Penn State, which I did," Canham recalled. "He didn't want to leave that program. Then, Sonny said, 'There's a guy at Miami who's pretty good.' Joe said the same thing. All I know was he had a long name and was supposed to be a good coach."

Canham said there was no way his next coach wouldn't be familiar with Ohio. It was too big and too fertile a recruiting area to let the Buckeyes have it to themselves.

Finally, the decision was made, after Schembechler had chances to take over at Wisconsin in 1967 and at Kansas State and Vanderbilt during his brief discussions with Canham.

Retired Michigan coach Bo Schembechler paces the sideline during the 2005 Rose Bowl as Michigan faced off against Texas. *Stephen Dunn/Getty Images*

Bo Schembechler celebrates Michigan's 22-14 victory over Southern California in the 1989 Rose Bowl in Pasadena, California. *Paul Jasienski/Getty Images*

"IF SCHEMBECHLER DIDN'T INVENT TOUGH LOVE, HE CERTAINLY SHOWED ITS POWER."

His starting salary? Try $21,000. It was the smartest decision either man or any school ever made. It was one of the most lucrative choices, too, in terms of long-term revenue.

When you consider the attendance for the 1967 OSU-Michigan game in Ann Arbor was just 64,144 and there hasn't been a crowd of less than 100,000 at Michigan Stadium since October 25, 1975, it's clear what Canham and Schembechler did.

There could've been another two zeroes on the original contract and Schembechler still would've been a bargain. The beauty then, and years later when he considered and rejected a big-bucks deal at Texas A&M, was that the money didn't seem to matter.

What mattered were people, especially his players. And if Schembechler didn't invent tough love, he certainly showed its power, beginning when he told the athletes on campus to prepare for the roughest months of their lives.

"Those who stayed" got exactly that. And it was only natural for them to wonder whether all the work was worth it in Schembechler's first months with the Wolverines.

After a blowout loss to Missouri and a rare defeat at Michigan State, one of just four defeats by the Spartans in a 21-year span, Michigan caught fire and rolled into the regular-season finale with a 7-2 record.

Their opponent, the supposedly unbeatable Buckeyes, were perfect again. And if Hayes didn't smile when he learned his disciple had moved to "That School Up North," he cried crocodile tears when the Wolverines were through with him on November 22, 1969.

"The Greatest Game in Michigan Football History" doesn't have a close competitor. Maybe it would've if Hayes hadn't gone for a pour-it-on, two-point conversion the year before, simply because "I couldn't go for three!" as he told assistant Lou Holtz.

With the Wolverines seething for 364 days and catching "Dr. Strangehayes" and his players a tad overconfident, Schembechler fired the shot that started "The 10-Year War."

By outworking and outplaying the Buckeyes for 60 minutes and winning the battles on offense, defense, and special teams, Michigan earned a 24-12 triumph as a 16-point underdog.

The Rose Bowl was a different story and the start of great frustration for the winningest program in college football history. When Schembechler suffered a heart attack hours before kickoff, the Jim Young-led Wolverines lost 10-3 to USC.

That brings us back to the numbers. And some of those stats mean more than a 2-8 mark in Pasadena or a 5-12 record in bowls ever could.

Let's start with 26 winning seasons in 27 tries and one .500 year when Schembechler's top two quarterbacks were injured. Or how about 17 bowl appearances in 21 chances at Michigan?

His four teams that stayed home were a combined 39-3-1 with three shared conference titles. But the Big Ten's Neanderthal policy of allowing just one team to play in a bowl, three heartbreaking finishes against OSU and the worst news he ever received made Schembechler even more determined.

When the 1973 showdown of unbeaten teams ended in a 10-10 tie, a game that saw the Buckeyes complete zero passes and the Wolverines finish without injured quarterback Dennis Franklin, the league's A.D.s voted 6-4 to send OSU back to the Rose Bowl.

"That was the maddest I've ever been," Schembechler said years later when accepting the Duffy Daugherty Memorial Award for outstanding contributions to college football. "It wasn't fair! What am I supposed to tell my kids? We should've been in that game! We weren't . . . and I'll never forget it!"

In fact, those Franklin-led teams from 1972-74 went 30-2-1 and never had the opportunity to play in a postseason game. They did earn Big Ten championship rings every season. And Schembechler made that the ultimate goal, not some mythical national title.

When the Wolverines beat OSU for the third straight year in 1978, no one knew a decade of Bo-vs.-Woody battles had ended. But after Hayes slugged Clemson linebacker Charlie Bauman in the Gator Bowl, he was fired before returning to Columbus.

Schembechler's record against Hayes was 5-4-1. Adding the nine games against Earle Bruce's squads and two more against John Cooper's OSU teams, his final mark against the Scarlet-and-Gray was 11-9-1.

Again, those numbers weren't as important as the boys he helped mature into men. If you talked to Schembechler in the last 25 years, it was never about the wins or losses, as insanely competitive as he seemed at the time. It was all about the players, the memories, and self-respect.

"We had great teams at Michigan," Schembechler said. "Am I proud of that? You bet I am! But there's a right way and wrong way to do things. We did things the right way here."

Michigan students attend a candlelight vigil on campus for beloved coach Bo Schembechler in Ann Arbor on Friday, November 17, 2006, the night of his passing. *AP/WWP*

The Wolverines did it The Schembechler Way. That meant you didn't cut corners. And you didn't cut classes. You cut your mistakes and gave your very best all day, every day. The best scoreboard was always the mirror.

When Schembechler had seen enough as a football coach, he handed the reins to Gary Moeller and succeeded Canham as A.D. It was there that he flashed his trademark temper again and struck another blow for loyalty, though it didn't end the way he planned.

After Michigan basketball coach Bill Frieder accepted the Arizona State job before the 1989 NCAA Tournament, Schembechler showed him the door and uttered the unforgettable line, "A Michigan man will coach Michigan!"

That badge of honor in Schembechler's eyes had nothing to do with academic degrees. Frieder had two from Michigan, two more than his boss. It was all about ethics and honesty. And the basketball program was a concern that way.

Schembechler's dream was to hire long-time friend Bob Knight to coach the Wolverines. After all, could a move from Indiana to Michigan in basketball generate more heat than he'd gotten for being a football "traitor" in Ohio?

At the 1989 Final Four in Seattle, Schembechler was seriously conflicted. He had appointed assistant coach Steve Fisher to lead the program in the NCAA Tournament. Six wins and a national title meant Fisher had earned a chance as head coach. But bringing Knight to Michigan was one of Schembechler's unfulfilled dreams.

Later, he scratched a baseball itch by becoming the president of the Detroit Tigers. When Schembechler took the hit for the firing of beloved broadcast icon Ernie Harwell,

no one remembered an emphasis on retooling the farm system or anything else.

As much as Schembechler loved baseball, it was a long way behind family, football, and Michigan on his list. When his wife, Millie, died of cancer, he became the best fund-raiser a cause ever had.

He became a firm believer in following orders for once. His cardiologist, Dr. Kim Eagle, called Schembechler "the most courageous patient I've ever met." Did he live beyond his time from strictly a medical standpoint? Not till he'd spoken to the Wolverines one last time.

Twenty-eight hours after passing away, Schembechler watched from a Skybox in heaven as Michigan met Ohio State for the 103rd time. He would've watched with his former boss if Canham could've sat still that long. Or he could've watched with Hayes, who surely would've shared his disgust with the game's 583 passing yards.

Instead, he probably sat with Tom Slade, who quarterbacked the Wolverines in 1971 and became a highly successful dentist. Schembechler wept at Slade's funeral one day before his own heart gave out. They're still on the same team. ✦

Jack Ebling, a three-time Michigan sportswriter of the year, was a 2006 inductee into the Greater Lansing Sports Hall of Fame. He has written five books—including Tales from the Detroit Tigers, *a February 2007 release—and won 21 major writing awards. After 25 years at the* Lansing State Journal, *he moved to talk radio and currently hosts "Ebling & You" on 1320 WILS-AM.*

CELEBRATING THE LIFE OF
BO SCHEMBECHLER
1929-2006

EXTRAORDINARY LOSS FOR COLLEGE FOOTBALL

NOVEMBER 18, 2006
BY LARRY LAGE, ASSOCIATED PRESS

IN THE END, MICHIGAN VS. OHIO STATE may have been too much for Bo Schembechler's failing heart.

The man with half-century-old roots to The Game died at age 77 on Friday on the eve of perhaps the biggest matchup in the storied rivalry's history, No 1 vs. No. 2, and his doctor said it might have been because of all the excitement.

Schembechler, who became one of college football's great coaches in two decades at Michigan, collapsed at the studios of WXYZ-TV in the Detroit suburb of Southfield, where he taped a weekly show. He was pronounced dead a little more than two hours later at nearby Providence Hospital.

"It's fair to say Bo wanted to live his life with vigor," said Dr. Kim Eagle, Schembechler's physician. "Ironically, he and I were going to see each other yesterday, but he wanted to address the team."

Could the stress of today's game have caused his death?

"I believe that's entirely possible," Eagle said.

Schembechler had a device that worked as a pacemaker and defibrillator implanted last month.

Doctors said he didn't have a heart attack Friday as much as his heart just quit working.

Schembechler had a heart attack on the eve of his first Rose Bowl in 1970 and another one in 1987, and had two quadruple heart-bypass operations. He also had diabetes.

"The fact that he lived to this day is nothing short of a miracle," Eagle said.

Schembechler played for Woody Hayes at Miami of Ohio, began his coaching career as a graduate

An impromptu memorial was constructed outside the University of Michigan's football practice facility, shortly after word of Bo Schembechler's death arrived on campus. *AP/WWP*

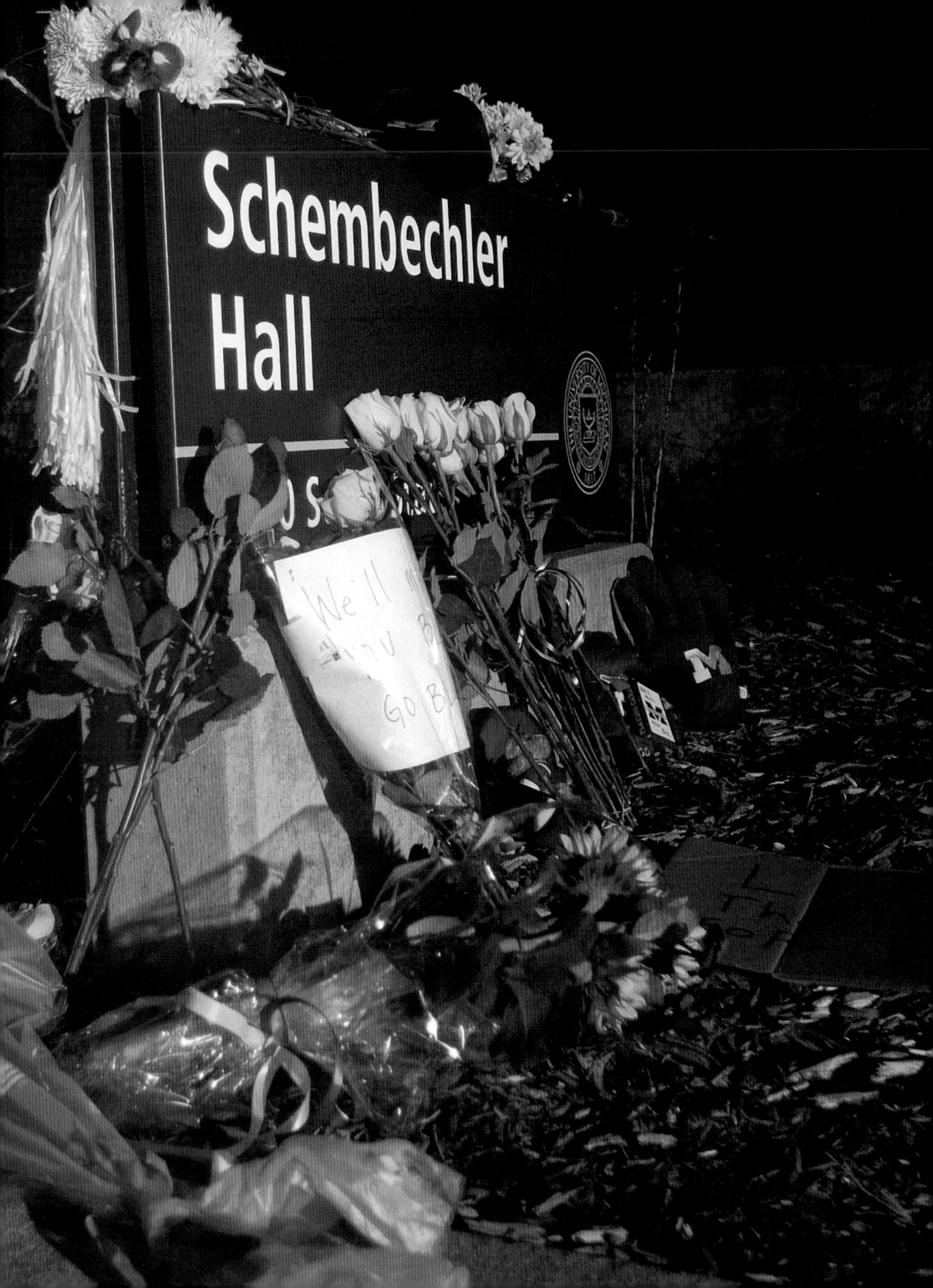
Schembechler
Hall

assistant for Hayes at Ohio State and then, in his first season at Michigan in 1969, knocked off Hayes' unbeaten Buckeyes.

"This is an extraordinary loss for college football," Ohio State coach Jim Tressel said in a statement. "Bo Schembechler touched the lives of many people and made the game of football better in every way. He will always be both a Buckeye and a Wolverine and our thoughts are with all who grieve his loss."

This year's Michigan players, who were toddlers when Schembechler's career was winding down in

"BO SCHEMBECHLER TOUCHED THE LIVES OF MANY PEOPLE AND MADE THE GAME OF FOOTBALL BETTER IN EVERY WAY."

—OHIO STATE COACH JIM TRESSEL

the late 1980s, were somber Friday afternoon as they left the building that bears his name and boarded buses for the 3 1/2-hour drive to Columbus, Ohio.

Michigan coach Lloyd Carr, who was hired by Schembechler in 1980, wiped a tear off his cheek as he sat in the front row of the first bus that left Ann Arbor.

"We have lost a giant at Michigan and in college football," Carr said in a statement. "There was never a greater ambassador for the University of Michigan, or college football, than Bo. Personally, I have lost a man I love."

A candlelight vigil for Bo Schembechler, attended mainly by students and staff, was held the night of his death on the Michigan campus. *AP/WWP*

Schembechler's health prevented him from traveling to road games in recent years, but he planned to watch the 103rd Michigan-Ohio State matchup at home.

A moment of silence is planned before the game.

Schembechler was a seven-time Big Ten coach of the year, compiling a 194-48-5 record at Michigan from 1969-89. His record in 26 years of coaching was 234-65-8. He never had a losing season.

"I'm not sure he has gotten his due as far as being one of the truly great football coaches of all time," Penn State coach Joe Paterno said. "I'm going to miss him."

Schembechler's Wolverines were 11-9-1 against the Buckeyes.

But fans in both states generally agree the rivalry's prime years were 1969-78, when Schembechler opposed his friend and coaching guru, Hayes. Michigan prevailed in those meetings, going 5-4-1.

In their first matchup, Schembechler's team pulled off a startling upset, winning 24-12 to deny No. 1 Ohio State its second consecutive national championship.

Thirteen of Schembechler's Michigan teams either won or shared the Big Ten championship. Seventeen of them finished in The Associated Press Top 10, with the 1985 team finishing No. 2.

Seventeen of Schembechler's 21 Michigan teams earned bowl berths. Despite a .796 regular-season winning percentage, his record in bowls was a disappointing 5-12, including 2-8 in Rose Bowls.

His last game as Wolverines coach was a 17-10 loss to Southern California in the 1990 Rose Bowl.

Schembechler is survived by a son, Glenn III, and his second wife, Cathy, whom he married in 1993. Schembechler's first wife, Millie, died in 1992. ✦

Bo Schembechler (center), "Wolfman" Don Dufek (left), and Gordon Bell begin preparation in Miami for their 1976 Orange Bowl game against Oklahoma. *AP/WWP*

Always animated on the sideline, Bo Schembechler protests a call late in the fourth quarter of a game against UCLA in 1982. *AP/WWP*

When Bo Schembechler arrived in Ann Arbor in the winter of 1968 to take over the head-coaching duties at Michigan, he brought with him a belief that to win in the Big Ten, a team had to be tough.

In his first spring as coach, Bo was intent on making Michigan tough. He put his team through one of the most grueling spring practices you can imagine. There was a lot of hitting and a lot of conditioning. None of us had been through this kind of work. It was physically difficult, and the mental pressure was just as intense.

Every day after practice we would drag ourselves into old Yost Field House to the locker room and collapse in front of our lockers. Survival was our goal, and some members of that first team didn't make it. Because of the tough work, there was a great deal of attrition.

Some would show up for practice, and looking ahead to the afternoon, they would just stare at their uniform, not get dressed, and quit the team. Others would come back after a particularly grueling day, slowly take off their uniform, shower, go back to their dorm, and never come back.

One of Bo's motivational techniques was to place signs throughout the locker room. One of our favorites was: "Those who stay will be champions."

One day after yet another rough practice, a group of guys were huddled around this particular sign and chuckling. As I worked my way close enough to see over the shoulder pads, I made out a magic marker scrawl under "Those who stay will be champions." It read, "Those who don't, will be doctors, lawyers, and other important people." At least one of our number who hadn't stayed left the rest of us something to smile about.

As you might guess, Bo immediately removed the magic marker scrawl and all was back in order.

Ultimately, though, Bo had the last laugh. The next fall, those who stayed through that difficult first spring were part of a Michigan team that upset Ohio State 24-12 in one of the great victories in Michigan football history. We went to the Rose Bowl as Big Ten champions.◆

From Jim Brandstatter's book, Tales from Michigan Stadium

MICHIGAN'S FINAL NATIONAL RANKINGS
UNDER BO

Year	AP	UPI	Year	AP	UPI
1969	9th	8th	1980	4th	4th
1970	9th	7th	1981	12th	12th
1971	6th	4th	1982	--	15th
1972	6th	6th	1983	8th	9th
1973	6th	6th	1984	--	--
1974	3rd	5th	1985	2nd	2nd
1975	8th	8th	1986	8th	7th
1976	3rd	3rd	1987	19th	18th
1977	9th	8th	1988	4th	4th
1978	5th	5th	1989	7th	8th
1979	18th	19th			

"HE WAS A FIREBALL. HE WAS FEISTY, A GREAT COMPETITOR. A GREAT MOTIVATOR OF HIS TEAMS. HE WAS AN OUTSTANDING COACH AND IT WAS SOMETHING TO SEE HIM AND WOODY GET AFTER IT THROUGH THE YEARS."

—FORMER OKLAHOMA COACH BARRY SWITZER

Michigan coach Bo Schembechler and Oklahoma coach Barry Switzer meet on the field prior to the 1976 Orange Bowl. Oklahoma went on to win the game 14-6. *Rich Clarkson/Sports Illustrated*

BO'S THOUGHTS ON OHIO STATE COACHING LEGEND WOODY HAYES

I LOVED WOODY HAYES.

That won't come as a surprise to many people because I've said it a couple zillion times. But dammit, it's a fact and I've never tried to hide it. After being associated with him for almost 40 years in one way or another, how could I feel any other way?

We had the greatest rivalry any two football coaches ever had, for ten glorious years. Man, did we compete! The sports writers called it a "war," and as far as the old man and I were concerned, it was.

You talk about tough ball games—Michigan vs. Ohio State games were. Every year but one, we battled for the Big Ten championship and the trip to the Rose Bowl, but the big thing was WINNING THE GAME!

Woody wanted to beat Michigan—and me—more than anything in the world, and you can believe that nothing got me as excited as beating Ohio State and the old man. What more could a couple football guys ever want?

But the more time goes by, the more I'm convinced that those ten years of intense rivalry and competition actually brought us closer together. I hate to do it or admit it, but I can get damned nostalgic and choked up when I think about Woody and those games and the wonderful relationship we had from the time I played for him at Miami University to the sad day he left us in 1987.

Woody Hayes was a unique individual, one that comes along only once. Believe me, I know, and I'm grateful for having shared so much of his life and for being in a position to appreciate his different perspectives and what a hell of a man he was.♦

From Bo's 1991 foreword to the authorized biography of Woody Hayes, Woody Hayes: A Reflection, authored by Paul Hornung

Bo Schembechler (left) and Ohio State coach Woody Hayes. Schembechler and his Wolverines were 5-4-1 against Hayes' Buckeyes. *AP/WWP*

Michael Taylor had grand dreams for college, and he believed Michigan coaches shared them. From the moment Michigan began to recruit [the former Wolverines quarterback] out of Cincinnati Princeton High School in 1984, Coach Bo Schembechler made it clear that no prospect was more important. In fact, Taylor says, Schembechler was so determined to bring him to Ann Arbor that he once told him he didn't trust anyone else on the staff to recruit him.

"I remember Bo called me from the locker room after they were embarrassed at Iowa, and he asked me if I had watched the game," Taylor said. "Then he said: 'Now you know why I need you.'" ◆

From Jim Cnockaert's book, Michigan: Where Have You Gone?

As Michigan and Texas prepare to face off in the 2005 Rose Bowl, their former head coaches—Bo Schembechler (right) and Darrell Royal—take questions from the media. *AP/WWP*

> "BO WAS LIKE A SECOND DAD TO ME. HIS LEGACY OF COACHING HAS REACHED THOUSANDS, AND WE ARE FORTUNATE TO HAVE BEEN TRAINED BY HIM. HE IS THE REASON I MADE IT TO THE NFL AND AS A HEAD FOOTBALL COACH. HE WAS A MAN OF INTEGRITY, A MAN OF HONESTY, AND A MAN OF CHARISMA, AND HE WILL BE REMEMBERED AS ONE OF THE GREAT TEACHERS AND WINNERS IN THE GAME FOR ALL-TIME."
>
> —FORMER MICHIGAN QUARTERBACK AND CURRENT UNIVERSITY OF SAN DIEGO COACH JIM HARBAUGH

Under the direction of head coach Chalmers "Bump" Elliott, Michigan's success in football was spotty and largely unspectacular from 1959 through 1968.

A Big Ten championship in 1964 and a Rose Bowl victory on New Years Day, 1965, was clearly the pinnacle for Bump's Wolverines.

Michigan's two biggest rivals—Michigan State and Ohio State—dominated the Maize and Blue in unprecedented fashion during that span. Duffy Daugherty's Spartans, a powerhouse in the 1960s, put together a record of 7-0-1 versus U-M at one stretch, while Woody Hayes' Buckeyes were 7-2.

Attendance rarely exceeded 70,000 in the Wolverines' massive 100,000-seat stadium, so it was undoubtedly time for a change. New athletic director Don Canham, with Elliott's assistance, began an immediate search and they soon targeted Miami of Ohio coach Bo Schembechler as their man. Bo had been tutored by such coaching legends as Woody Hayes at Ohio State and Ara Parseghian at Northwestern, and had built the Redskins into a Mid-American

Bo Schembechler waits in the tunnel with his team prior to the 1990 Rose Bowl against the USC Trojans. *Mike Powell/Getty Images*

Conference power as head coach. He was quietly confident that he was ready for Big Ten competition.

In John McCallum's book, *Big Ten Football*, he wrote that Canham was overwhelmed by Schembechler's charisma and enthusiasm during their initial interview. A day later, the Michigan athletic director told Bo the job was his:

"Good," said Bo.

"Fine," said Canham, "the salary is $21,000."

That was only about a thousand more than Bo would have earned at Miami, but money was never a major factor for him in the decision. The challenge of competition was the driving force.

McCallum wrote that Schembechler was bluntly honest with Canham.

"There's no way I'm going to be a winner right off the bat," Bo said. "You may as well know that right now."

"I know it," Canham said.

"Then how long do I have to build a winner?" Bo asked.

"Five years," Canham told him. "Take my word for it."

"Well," said Bo, "be patient with me, because anything can happen."

It took only a year for Schembechler to show U-M fans that something special was right around the bend. ◆

BO'S NFL FIRST-ROUND DRAFT PICKS

1972 ... **THOM DARDEN,** CLEVELAND BROWNS

1972 ... **MIKE TAYLOR,** NEW YORK JETS

1973 ... **PAUL SEYMOUR,** BUFFALO BILLS

1974 ... **DAVE GALLAGHER,** CHICAGO BEARS

1975 ... **DAVE BROWN,** PITTSBURGH STEELERS

1978 ... **MIKE KENN,** ATLANTA FALCONS

1978 ... **JOHN ANDERSON,** GREEN BAY PACKERS

1979 ... **JON GIESLER,** MIAMI DOLPHINS

1980 ... **CURTIS GREER,** ST. LOUIS CARDINALS

1981 ... **MEL OWENS,** LOS ANGELES RAMS

1982 ... **BUTCH WOOLFOLK,** NEW YORK GIANTS

1985 ... **KEVIN BROOKS,** DALLAS COWBOYS

1987 ... **JIM HARBAUGH,** CHICAGO BEARS

"BO SCHEMBECHLER HAD A NEVER-GIVE-UP ATTITUDE. THAT WAS HIS PHILOSOPHY, AND IT IS MY PHILOSOPHY. IF YOU SET GOALS AND WORK HARD ENOUGH, YOU CAN ACHIEVE SUCCESS. I BELIEVE IN OUR OLD TEAM MOTTO, THAT THOSE WHO STAY WILL BE CHAMPIONS. I AM STILL A CHAMPION IN MY OWN MIND, ESPECIALLY WHEN I WALKED ACROSS THAT STAGE AND HEARD THEM ANNOUNCE 'DR. WILLIAM TAYLOR.' THAT WAS THE GREATEST PERSONAL ACHIEVEMENT IN MY LIFE. THAT WAS MY BEST MOMENT SINCE I SCORED THAT [1971] TOUCH-DOWN AGAINST OHIO STATE."

—FORMER MICHIGAN TAILBACK BILLY TAYLOR, FROM THE BOOK MICHIGAN: WHERE HAVE YOU GONE?

AP/WWP

BO VS. BIG TEN TEAMS (1969-1989)

VS. ILLINOIS ... 19-1-1

VS. INDIANA ... 16-1

VS. IOWA ... 13-3-1

VS. MICHIGAN STATE ... 17-4

VS. MINNESOTA ... 19-2

VS. NORTHWESTERN ... 14-0

VS. OHIO STATE ... 11-9-1

VS. PURDUE ... 16-3

VS. WISCONSIN ... 18-1

During the 1990 Rose Bowl, Bo Schembechler and assistant coach Gary Moeller send in instructions from the sideline. The game was Schembechler's last in a career that spanned 27 years. *AP/WWP*

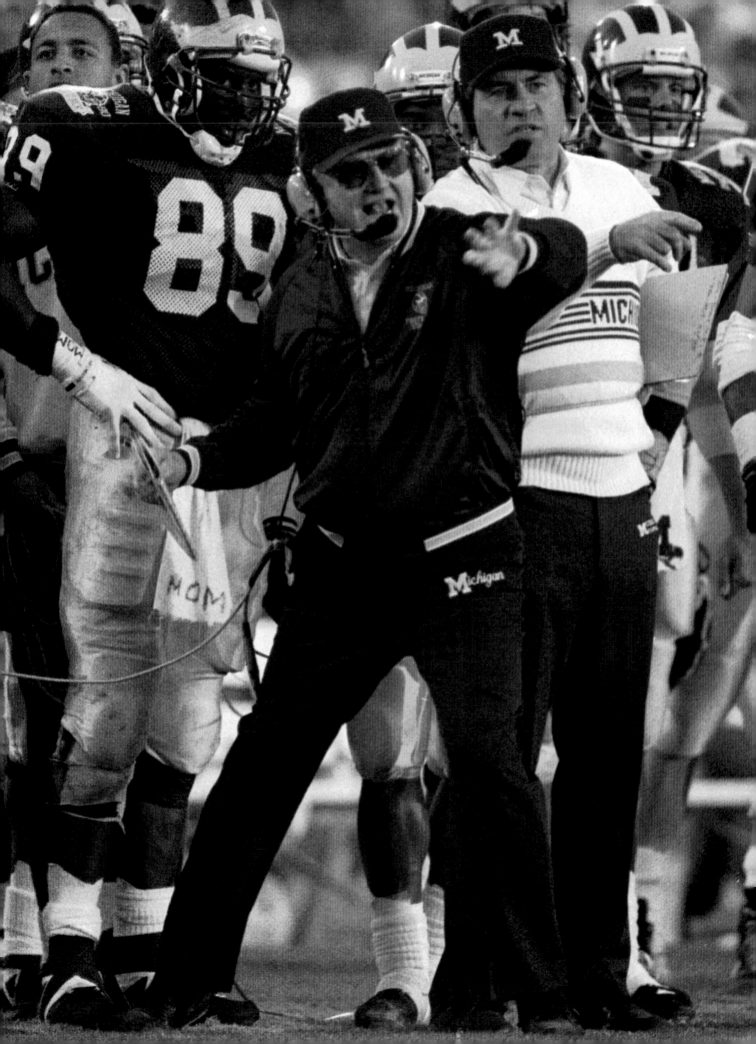

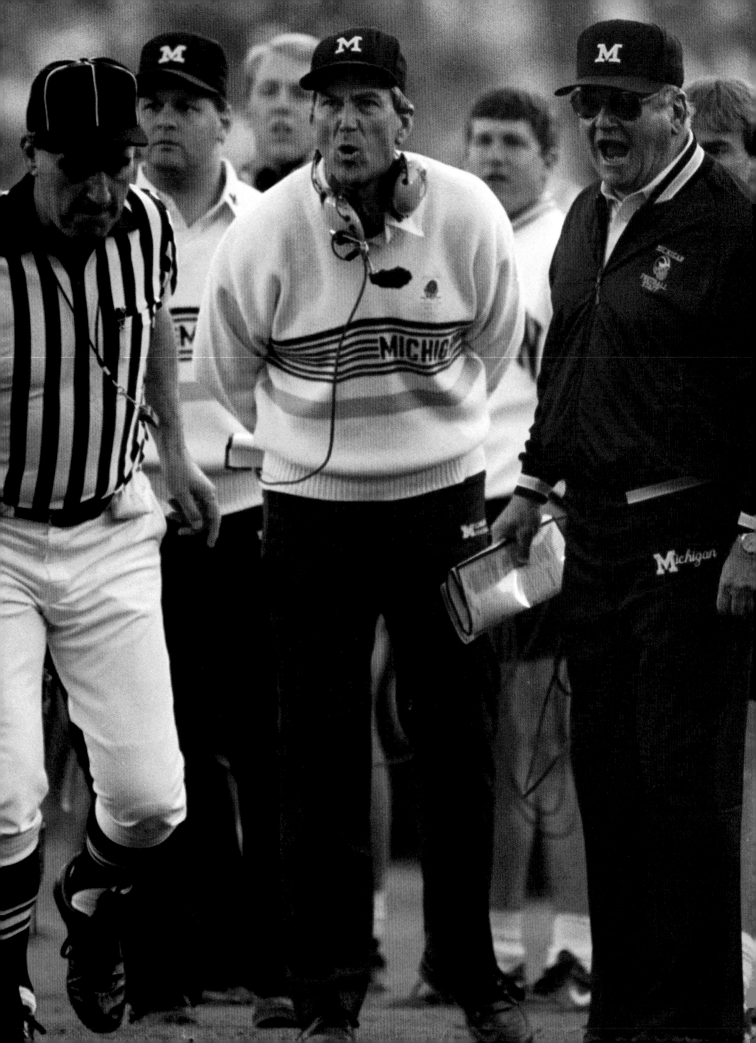

Jerry Hanlon and Bo Schembechler have been through a lot in their days at Michigan, and Hanlon is a great source of information regarding Bo's legendary volcanic personality. This story is about one of those eruptions. Surprisingly, according to Hanlon, this outburst contained no four-letter words. It wasn't uttered above a normal speaking voice, yet Jerry tells me that it was the worst thing he ever heard Bo say to a referee.

"The truth of the matter," Hanlon says, "Bo very seldom hollered at officials. He would talk to them when an official walked close to the bench. That was when he would get on officials. To holler out at them on the field, I don't remember him doing a lot of that. It was when they got close to the sideline is when he would let them know what he felt about certain things in no uncertain terms.

"The best one, though," Jerry continued with a smile, "wasn't in our stadium. We were on the road at Wisconsin one year and we were walking off the field after the game. Bo was so mad at one of the officials. You've got to understand, the officiating was bad. We were all mad. Anyway, we were walking off the field and this official was walking in front of us. Bo said, 'You walk like a girl!'"

Hanlon laughs out loud at the memory of that one. "I thought that was the worst thing he could have said, but that was his comment. It was the biggest put-down I may have ever heard from him to an official." ✦

From Jim Brandstatter's book, Tales from Michigan Stadium

An always animated Bo Schembechler (right) and assistant coach Lloyd
Carr vociferously disagree with a Rose Bowl referee's call. *AP/WWP*

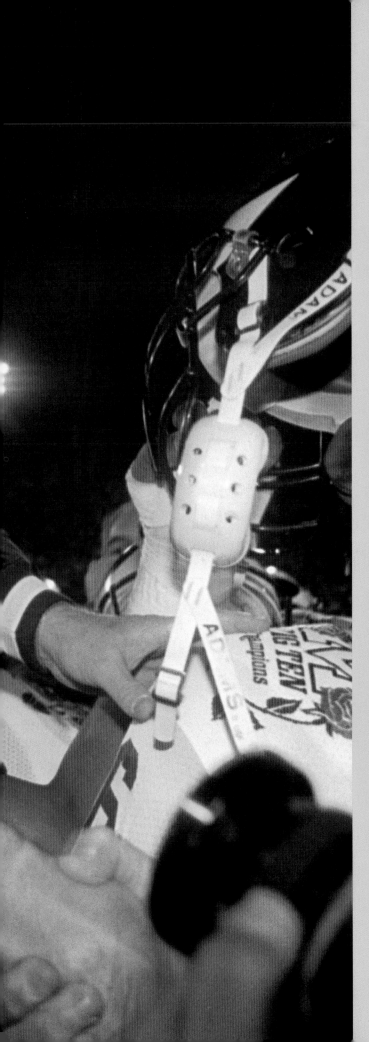

"[BO] WAS A GIANT OF A COACH AND GIANT OF A MAN. HIS LIFE TOUCHED GENERATIONS OF PLAYERS, FAMILIES, STAFF, STUDENTS AND ALUMNI. HIS ENERGY FUELED NOT ONLY ATHLETIC SUCCESS BUT THE INCREDIBLE PRIDE OF ALL MICHIGAN FANS. HIS IMPACT WAS IMMEASURABLE."

—MICHIGAN ATHLETIC DIRECTOR BILL MARTIN

Bo Schembechler is carried on the shoulders of his players after Michigan defeated Southern California 22-14 in the 1989 Rose Bowl. *AP/WWP*

BO'S MICHIGAN PLAYERS IN HEISMAN TROPHY BALLOTING

1974 ... Dennis Franklin (8th)

1975 ... Gorden Bell (8th)

1976 ... Rob Lytle (3rd)

1977 ... Rick Leach (8th)

1978 ... Rick Leach (3rd)

1980 ... Anthony Carter (10th)

1981 ... Anthony Carter (7th)

1982 ... Anthony Carter (4th)

1986 ... Jim Harbaugh (3rd)

After defeating Ohio State in 1969, Bo Schembechler is swept from the field on the shoulders of his team. *Tony Tomsic/Sports Illustrated*

Those who played for Bo Schembechler have a wealth of tales to tell about Bo. Whenever we have reunions, we always have a great time telling each other what we affectionately call "Bo stories." Schembechler claims that we embellish these tales way too much. He swears he didn't do half the things we say he did. While he may be correct in some instances, there are others that he knows are true, and this is one of them.

In Bo's first year at Michigan, we were preparing for a game late in the season. During the week of the game we had a terrible snowstorm in Ann Arbor, and everything was covered in snow, including our practice field. All day long, the players had wondered where we would practice that day. Back then, there was no indoor practice facility with artificial turf. The only place we had to practice indoors was Yost Field House. The prospect of practicing in Yost on the hard dirt surface and cinders was not very pleasant. We were all kind of curious what Bo would do that day, considering Mother Nature's assault on his practice schedule.

When we got to Yost in the afternoon to dress and get ready for practice, we heard rumors that the assistant coaches, managers, and some freshmen had been out on the practice field shoveling snow. We couldn't imagine that Bo was really considering going outside, but we weren't sure. We had seen him do some things we hadn't seen done before, so we all got ready as if it were a normal day. In the back of our minds, though, we thought indoors would be the choice.

As we all started our march down the stairs to the door leading from Yost to the outside and practice, we were told to wait. At that point, we figured Bo had made his decision, and we would be practicing indoors. We gathered around in groups. Some stretched; some just stood talking. We were waiting for Bo to appear. He hadn't been around from the time we had arrived to dress for practice.

Finally, the small door to Yost flew open, and Bo strode in wearing his Michigan hat and a heavy coat. Snow was sticking to him. He yelled, "Bring it up, men!"

We gathered in a big circle around him. He said, "It's pretty rough weather out there. But remember what Admiral King said to his troops in World War II: 'If you're going to fight in the North Atlantic, you've got to train in the North Atlantic!' Ok, now let's go!"

With that, Bo turned and ran to the door and into the elements outside. We all roared and followed him into the wind and snow. None of us knew who Admiral King was, and we had no clue whether Admiral King had ever said such a thing, but we practiced two hours outside on a field that had been shoveled semi-clean.

The following Saturday, we played on the road in cold conditions. As I recall, there wasn't a lot of snow, maybe a few flurries during the game, but we won handily. We never questioned again whether we would practice indoors or outdoors. Bo had made his point. If he was going to take his team to play in the snow, he was certainly going to make his team practice in it, too.

Thank you, Admiral King! ◆

From Jim Brandstatter's book, Tales from Michigan Stadium

"I REALLY HAD GREAT ADMIRATION FOR BO.
HE WAS SUCH A STRAIGHT GUY. YOU
ALWAYS KNEW WHERE YOU STOOD WITH
HIM. HE WAS DIRECT AND HONEST, A GEN-
UINE FOOTBALL MAN. HE COACHED THE
WAY YOU ARE SUPPOSED TO PLAY THE GAME,
WHICH IS HARD-NOSED."

—FORMER NEBRASKA COACH TOM OSBORNE

AP/WWP

"[BO] WAS JUST FUN TO BE AROUND AND
YOU JUST COULDN'T HELP BUT COME AWAY
INSPIRED BECAUSE HE JUST HAD A GREAT
WAY ABOUT HIM. SOMEBODY SAID, 'HOW
WOULD YOU DESCRIBE HIM?' HE WAS HIS
OWN MAN."

— FORMER NOTRE DAME AND SOUTH CAROLINA
COACH LOU HOLTZ

MICHIGAN REMEMBERS A 'GIANT OF A COACH'

NOVEMBER 17, 2006
BY TOM KRISHER, ASSOCIATED PRESS

IT PROBABLY WAS HARD for Bo Schembechler to sit in a sophomore-level class called Systematic Thinking About Problems of the Day and not get involved in the discussion.

But day after day this semester, the feisty old coach who always had an opinion would take a seat and listen to discussions about the electoral college, the propriety of downloading music from the Internet and the impact of globalization on the U.S. economy.

"That he was part of the university really meant a lot to him," said Paul Courant, the professor and former provost at the University of Michigan.

Even though he had not coached a game since 1990, Schembechler's fiery presence was always felt across the Ann Arbor campus, where his death on Friday cast a gloomy shadow on the eve of one of the biggest football games in university history.

University President Mary Sue Coleman called the death a "tremendous shock" and an "irreplaceable loss" for the school.

"He was a giant of a coach and a giant of a man," Michigan athletic director Bill Martin said at a news conference at the hospital where Schembechler died at 77.

To many, it seemed like Schembechler was always around, and that he always would be. He spoke to freshman athletes, telling them about the responsibilities that came with wearing a Michigan uniform. He

Bo Schembechler's team carries him from the field on their shoulders after another victory over Ohio State.
John Iacono/Sports Illustrated

"THAT HE WAS PART OF THE UNIVERSITY REALLY MEANT A LOT TO HIM."

—PAUL COURANT, PROFESSOR AND FORMER PROVOST AT THE UNIVERSITY OF MICHIGAN

gave pep talks to the football team. He used his iconic status to help raise money, recently at the newly built Gerald R. Ford School of Public Policy.

Schembechler took Public Policy 201 because of his interest in current issues, Courant said, and he attended consistently. He didn't talk because he preferred to listen to the students.

"He told me often he was impressed a lot about how much they knew and how willing they were to mix it up, to make an argument," Courant said.

He gave his opinions after class to Courant and the teaching assistants.

Schembechler attended his last class on Tuesday, and seemed fine even though it was just weeks after an earlier hospitalization for heart troubles, Courant said.

Sophomore water polo player Mary Chatigny, 19, of Palm Springs, Calif., had never heard of Schembechler until she came to Michigan. But she was inspired when he spoke at a banquet for all freshmen athletes, telling them what it means to wear a Michigan uniform.

"Always hold yourself in responsibility. Be proud to wear your Michigan gear. Be proud to be a student-athlete," she remembers him saying.

He also told them to go to class and always be on time, something her parents often told her.

"Coming from him, it just stuck so much more," she said.

She called the timing of the death, the day before the game between No. 1 Ohio State and No. 2 Michigan, "surreal," but thought it would inspire the Wolverines.

Bo Schembechler, surrounded by Michigan players and fans, hoists the 1989 Rose Bowl trophy. Michigan defeated USC 22-14. *AP/WWP*

Since 1969, Ann Arbor barber Jerry Erickson has cut Schembechler's hair once a month—except when the former coach wintered in Florida. He was in the shop shortly before he became ill Oct. 20, and Erickson said he seemed just as feisty as ever.

After the cut was finished, Erickson followed Schembechler to the street, shook his hand and said, "Hey Bo, you've got my Ohio State tickets." Erickson recalled Schembechler's reply. He said the coach profanely told him the only thing he had for him was a good swift kick.

At the main entrance to Michigan Stadium, two bouquets of yellow roses were stuck in the wrought-iron fence, some maize and blue balloons were tied near them and a sign was posted that said: "We will miss you Bo. M Go Blue."

To Courant, Schembechler's passing means the end to one of the greatest pleasures of returning to teaching after years as an administrator. He loved talking football with the coach, who on Tuesday, in what would be their last conversation, asked Courant who would win the big game.

Courant said Michigan because its linemen are stronger on both sides of the ball.

"He said, 'Yeah, I think so, too,'" Courant said. ✦

An autographed picture of Bo Schembechler hangs on the wall at the Coach & Four barbershop in Ann Arbor. Owner Jerry Erickson cut Schembechler's hair once a month since 1969—except when the former coach wintered in Florida. *AP/WWP*

John Biever/Sports Illustrated

"I REMEMBER BO AS THE CONSUMMATE TEAM PER-
SON. HE PREACHED IT, HE BELIEVED IT. HE DIDN'T
TALK ABOUT STARS. HE HAD A TEAM, ON THE
FIELD, IN THE OFFICE, AND EVERYBODY WORKED
FOR A COMMON GOAL. AND I THINK THAT'S
WHAT ENDEARED HIM TO SO MANY PEOPLE. ... HE
EMBODIED LOYALTY. HE LED NOT OUT OF FEAR,
BUT OUT OF RESPECT AND LOVE. THAT'S WHY
PEOPLE BOUGHT INTO WHAT HE PREACHED."

—FORMER MICHIGAN AND CURRENT SAN DIEGO STATE
BASKETBALL COACH STEVE FISHER

REMEMBERING "COACH BO"

BY JOHN HUMENIK
FORMER UNIVERSITY OF MICHIGAN
SPORTS INFORMATION DIRECTOR

On November 16, 2006, while flying home from some business meetings in the Midwest, I started to work on addressing envelopes for Christmas cards that I wanted to send out in the next few weeks. The final envelope I addressed before my plane landed in Jacksonville, Florida was to:

Coach Bo Schembechler
Athletics Department
University of Michigan
1000 South State
Ann Arbor, MI 48109

Today, November 17, I heard about his death on the day before perhaps the biggest Michigan-Ohio State game of all time. I was blessed during my 25 years as a sports information and communications director to work with some really high-profile people in college athletics: Princeton's Pete Carril; Bill Arnsparger, Emmitt Smith, Steve Spurrier, and Danny Wuerffel at the University of Florida. All fit into that category, but "Coach Bo" was truly a larger-than-life figure.

When you work in sports public relations, you come across many people whose public and media image is more positive than what you see or experience in private. I found "Coach Bo" to be one of those people who was quite a bit different than portrayed, but in a positive rather than negative way. He was fiercely loyal to his coaching staff, his players, and Michigan. Yes, he was tough and set in his ways, but I saw and experienced a side of him that I have, and always will, remember and treasure. That is one of the reasons why I always sent him a Christmas card. I never wanted him to forget that I will always remember him and the high standards he stood for and the excellence he demanded and inspired, and the impact he had on my own professional standards as a result.

As I addressed the Christmas card to him last night I found myself thinking, as I always did when I thought about him, of certain images and memories that make me smile and laugh.

I arrived at the University of Michigan on the Saturday before the first game of the 1980 season. I had not met Coach during my interview process as he was away on a trip, so I was anxious to meet him. As soon as I arrived in Ann Arbor I went straight to the stadium where the Wolverines were conducting their final fall squad scrimmage before the season opener. I was standing on the sideline watching the team warm up and Coach Bo was walking around with a yardstick. Don Canham, Michigan's Athletics Director, came over to me to welcome me aboard and as we were talking I mentioned to him that if possible I would appreciate it if he could introduce me to Coach.

At that very moment I heard this loud noise and looked out onto the field and saw Coach whacking several of the offensive linemen on the butt as he was not happy with their technique. Don looked at me at that moment and said, "I don't think this is a good time," and we both had a good laugh.

A couple of days later I was asked to speak at an alumni function in Ann Arbor, which Coach was present at, and I repeated this story. There was no one who laughed harder than Bo, and I can't tell you how good it made me feel when I saw that. Later that day he would tell me how much he respected me for telling that story when I had no idea how he would react, and that it showed him a quality about me that he liked. That was my first indication that his public and private persona were quite different.

A few months later, after a rather dismal 1-2 start to the season, the Wolverines rolled into Columbus with a seven-game win streak and the Big Ten title once again on the line with the Buckeyes. On the Saturday morning of the game, the team and staff arose to find that there was no hot water in the hotel. Of course Bo, like any football coach does who is looking for a motivational edge, used the incident to convey an image with the team that it was part of some conspiracy by Buckeye faithful to help their team and it showed a lack of respect for Michigan.

On the field about an hour before the game I visited with him and wished him luck and I saw that he had that twinkle in his eye that I came to realize over the previous two months meant that he was seeing and feeling something he liked. After the game, a rousing Wolverine win that sent the team to the Rose Bowl as Big Ten Champions, I will never forget him accepting a bouquet of roses from the Rose Bowl queen in the locker room and apologizing to her in private for how foul it smelled in the room, but it was due to the fact that "The damn Buckeyes saw to it that we could not take showers this morning."

On the day before the 1981 New Year's Rose Bowl vs. Washington, the Michigan team had a short practice at the Rose Bowl venue in Pasadena. While the team was dressing I walked back onto the field and sat down on the team bench and was thinking about all of the things that had transpired in my life the past few months since arriving from Princeton as well as taking in the vivid beauty of the sun shinning on the San Gabriel Mountains and the immaculate playing surface in this most famous venue. As I was sitting there and thinking about things, I felt an arm across my shoulder and looked up to see Coach Bo. He said, "What are you thinking about, young man?"

So I told him how I could not believe that I was here and all of the things that had taken place in my life in the last four months. He sat down next me, put his arm around me again, and said, "You know, I don't totally understand what you SID guys do, but I do know that whatever it is that you have done has made a difference. This season was the most organized media relations effort I've been a part of since I've been at Michigan. I always came out here to the Rose Bowl and felt like I was being pulled every which way and that we were always reacting to things, but this year it has not been that way, so whatever it is that you are doing, keeping doing it!"

To say that made me feel like a million dollars was an understatement. To this day it stands as perhaps the most meaningful professional compliment I ever got because I came to realize how high his standards were and the level of excellence he expected and demanded. I remember thinking that I felt he was sincere in what he was saying. I would find out two months later just how truly sincere he was with his feelings that day.

Michigan staff members Mary and Paul Guttman attend a candlelight vigil for former Michigan football coach Bo Schembechler in Ann Arbor on November 17, 2006, the day of his death. *AP/WWP*

Ann Arbor resident Ralph Hale stops at a makeshift memorial for Bo Schembechler adorning the south entrance gates to Michigan Stadium. *AP/WWP*

The next day, New Years Day 1981, Michigan beat Washington in the Rose Bowl, giving Coach his first win in that game since he became coach at Michigan in 1969. He had taken *so* much criticism for not winning the Rose Bowl. To see him *so* happy on the field and in the locker room after the game is something I'll never forget along with the memory of him leading the team in "Hail to the Victors" in the locker room after the game. Seeing him with a cigar in hand and standing on a bench leading the team in that storied collegiate fight song was, and is, so memorable. He was *so* happy, and the players, assistant coaches, and staff were *so* happy for him. I was blessed to have the opportunity to be in many locker rooms after many outstanding victories, but the atmosphere in that Rose Bowl venue ranks as the most special of them all.

A few hours after that Rose Bowl win, a production assistant for NBC's *Today Show* came to the team hotel and sought me out to say that she was there to finalize details for Coach Bo and Butch Woolfolk, the Rose Bowl's MVP, to appear on that show the next morning. I told her that I did not think that this was something that Coach would want to do, and she then pulled out some correspondence that showed that it was required, as per NBC's agreement with the Rose Bowl, that the winning coach and MVP were to appear

on this show. She informed me that Coach and Butch were to appear on the show at 7:45 a.m. ET, which was 4:45 a.m. California time and that we would be picked up at the hotel at 3:30 a.m. to be taken to the studio.

To say that I did not want to take this request to Coach Bo was an understatement, but I had to, even though I knew I would most likely be upsetting him after a most memorable and positive day. When I relayed this to him he was not happy, to say the least, and when he heard at what time he had to do this he became even more upset. In short, he said he was not going to do it, and I did my best to say, "Coach, don't let this become a story, a negative story. You have been great out here all week, you won the game, there is a good deal of positive stuff being written and said. Don't give people a chance to jump on the fact that you refused to do something that was contractually required."

It didn't work, and as I started to walk away thinking about how I was going to handle this with the NBC folks, he opened his hotel door and said, "John, tell them I'll do it if they let us park in Johnny Carson's space at the NBC Studio." Before I could say anything, he shut the door.

I did not have the nerve to knock on the door again so I relayed that request to the NBC rep and she made some calls and eventually told me that they have been able to get this done, not an easy matter on the evening of New Year's Day. She said that Johnny's parking spot was a pretty good distance from the actual studio the interview would be conducted, but that they would have some golf carts pick us up and take us over. They also would arrange for some photos to be taken of Coach and Butch during their complete visit to NBC.

Michigan fans and players carry a victorious Bo Schembechler from the field in Columbus, Ohio, after the Wolverines defeated Ohio State in 1978. *Tony Tomsic/Sports Illustrated*

So I went back to Coach's room and told him that all had been worked out in this regard, including the fact that he could get some photos taken, and he just started laughing and eventually told me that he was just kidding and had planned all along to do the interview when he had been made aware of it a couple of days earlier by Don Canham. He could not stop laughing and then went down the hallway knocking on the doors of some the assistant coaching saying, "I'm going to get to park in Johnny Carson's parking space. Do you believe it!" He was like a 20-year-old frat boy. It still brings a big smile to my face every time I think of that scene.

A few hours later, at 3:30 a.m, an NBC driver and limo picked up Coach, Butch, and me at the hotel to take us to NBC, and sure enough we parked in Johnny Carson's spot. Bo was instructing the photographer on the pictures he wanted taken. What a sight that was. We then went over to the *Today Show* studio where Bryant Gumble conducted the interview.

sorry for putting me through the thing with NBC last night, but he only did it because he thought I could take it, and he only played practical jokes on people he liked, and he laughed like only he could laugh.

When we arrived back in Ann Arbor after the Rose Bowl, Athletics Director Don Canham informed me that I would not be receiving a Rose Bowl ring. He explained that there was a certain amount of budgeted money for this award, and that there were so many people he wanted to give one to, most of whom had been there much longer than the four months I had. I totally understood and did not have any problems or issues with that decision.

In early March I set up a meeting with Coach Bo to get some things done regarding the spring prospectus for the 1981 season and team, and as we were discussing things when Bo said, "Why aren't you wearing your Rose Bowl ring?" I explained to him what Don Canham had relayed in January and he said, "That's bull. I'll get this strengthened up right now."

"[COACH BO] REALLY BELIEVED IN THE VALUES

OF COLLEGE ATHLETICS AND FOOTBALL."

It was around 5 a.m. local time as we were getting back into the limo, and Coach Bo said, "Lets go to breakfast. It's too late to sleep."

I can still see Butch rolling his eyes, because he wanted to go back to sleep. As we got into the limo, Coach said to the driver, "Take us to some breakfast place. I don't want one of those fancy Hollywood places. Take us to some local hole-in-the-wall place." The driver did just that. We went down more side streets than you can imagine, and when we pulled up to it—a real dump if you asked Butch and me—Coach said, "This is perfect!"

Once again, I'll never forget Butch rolling his eyes. So we went inside, where nobody knew Bo, and for the next 90 minutes Bo smoked a cigar, had a big breakfast, put his feet up on the table and read all of the local papers' reports on the Rose Bowl. His happiness and contentment were so obvious, and I remember thinking how happy I was for him and how blessed I was to share those special moments. When we were walking back to the car, he told me he was

I remember thinking, "Oh no! He is going to call Mr. Canham and make a big deal about this, and I'm going to get into trouble about it. I didn't want Don to think I was making a big deal about it."

But before I could say that, Coach Bo was on the phone calling the equipment manager and telling him to get to the office right away and to bring the ring measurement pieces with him. A few moments later that person arrived, and Coach Bo told him to measure me for a ring, get it made, and to charge him for payment. I was truly speechless and when I did try to say something he said, "I don't want to hear anything from you about this, and I don't want you to tell anyone. I want to do this. I told you at the Rose Bowl what I think about the job you are doing and this is my way of showing you I truly appreciate what you have done. Plus, this is further payback for the prank I played on you with the NBC stuff at the Rose Bowl!"

That gesture is one that ranked at the very top of my professional sports PR career. I was blessed to receive several conference championships, bowl

Michigan coach Bo Schembechler (right) meets with Ohio State coach Earl Bruce prior to their game in Columbus.
Paul Jasienski/Getty Images

game, and even one national championship ring while at Florida, but that Rose Bowl ring means the most because of what Coach Bo did to make sure I received one. Whenever I look at it, it totally reminds me of a person who so many others never saw. It always made me, and still wants to make me, tell people of a Bo Schembechler who was a good deal different from his public image.

I'm so thankful for these and other memories. Throughout my professional career whenever I was asked, "What was Coach Schembechler really like?" I was always glad to use that opportunity to tell them that I found him to be a very caring person, a person who had a very kind heart if he believed you were loyal to the things he stood for and believed in and

were loyal to him, his coaching staff, and Michigan. I was glad to tell them that he was a coach with a staff and group of players who were fiercely loyal to him because they knew he was fiercely loyal to them. That he was a man and coach who really believed in the values of college athletics and football. That he was a man and coach who helped make college football a better sport. That he was a man with a high level of honesty, integrity, and rock-solid beliefs in certain ideals. I'm glad to tell them he was one of those rare individuals who had an ability to inspire excellence. I'm always glad to tell them that he was a man who made a life-long impression on me in a very positive way, and that he was a man and coach who truly did cast a bigger than life figure and shadow. ✦

A native of Schembechler's hometown of Barberton, Ohio, [tailback] Lawrence Ricks chose Michigan as much for academic as for athletic reasons. On his official visit to Ann Arbor, Schembechler introduced him to the dean of the School of Engineering. When Ricks and his father met later with Schembechler, the coach explained how he would be successful as a college student, not just as a football player. "Coach (Joe) Paterno was very similar at Penn State," Ricks recalled. "[Bo] didn't sell football as much as he talked about how you fit into the school and his program." ✦

From Jim Cnockaert's book, Michigan:Where Have You Gone?

"BO SCHEMBECHLER WAS AN OUTSTANDING CITIZEN IN EVERY RESPECT. HE WAS A DEAR FRIEND OF OURS AND WILL BE GREATLY MISSED BY HIS NUMEROUS FRIENDS. IT IS A GREAT LOSS TO THE UNIVERSITY OF MICHIGAN IN PARTICULAR AND FOOTBALL IN GENERAL."

—FORMER U.S. PRESIDENT GERALD R. FORD, WHO PLAYED CENTER ON THE MICHIGAN FOOTBALL TEAM IN THE 1930s

BO'S ALL-AMERICANS AT MICHIGAN

Tom Curtis, S, 1969
Jim Mandich, E, 1969
Dan Dierdorf, OT, 1970
Henry Hill, MG, 1970
Marty Huff, LB, 1970
William Taylor, HB, 1971
Randy Logan, DB, 1972
Paul Seymour, OT, 1972
David Gallagher, DT, 1973
Dave Brown, DB, 1973-74
Don Dufek, DB, 1975
Mark Donahue, OG, 1976-77
John Anderson, LB, 1977
Walt Downing, C, 1977
Rick Leach, QB, 1978
Curtis Greer, DT, 1979
Ron Simpkins, LB, 1979
William "Bubba" Paris, OT, 1981
Harold "Butch" Woolfolk, TB, 1981
Anthony Carter, WR, 1980-81-82
Tom Dixon, C, 1983
Stefan Humphries, OG, 1983
Brad Cochran, DB, 1985
Mike Hammerstein, DT, 1985
Jim Harbaugh, QB, 1986
Garland Rivers, DB, 1986
John "Jumbo" Elliott, OT, 1986-87
Mark Messner, DT, 1987-88
John Vitale, C, 1988
Tripp Welborne, S, 1989

Because he played for Woody Hayes at Miami of Ohio and later coached under him at Ohio State, Bo Schembechler became known as "Little Woody" when he assumed the head coaching job at Michigan in 1969.

The epithet was undeserved. Oh, Bo could growl and throw temper tantrums like Woody, but he was basically a good guy. You could needle Bo back and he could take it as well as dish it out.

In the 1970s, the American Football Coaches Association had a tie-in with the Tea Council of the U.S.A. Every spring, a different head coach would come to New York and we'd visit for a spell.

Bo was the visiting coach one year and we went for a drink (something other than tea, as I recall) at the Top of the Sixes, an establishment atop a skyscraper at 666 Fifth Avenue. It was the year after Michigan lost four games directly attributable to breakdowns in the kicking game.

As we sat down, Bo looked at me and needled, "You know, you write some of the most horseshit stories I've ever read."

"That may be," I replied, "but I've never had a story blocked."

Bo's 1984 Michigan team, which had a mediocre 6-5 record, played 11-0 and top-ranked Brigham Young in the Holiday Bowl. It rained in San Diego much of that late-December week and it was actually colder there than in Buffalo, N.Y. The *San Diego Union* ran a box on the front page every day to prove it.

Bo and the Wolverines arrived on a wet Tuesday for a Friday night game. Bo was an hour or so late to a press conference, and when he arrived, BYU coach LaVell Edwards said, "Welcome to San Diego."

"Aaarrrggghhh," Bo growled, "it's your home game, isn't it? (the Western Athletic Conference champion was the host team.) How come every time we go to a bowl we're always the visiting team? (the Pac-10 team was always considered the host team in the Rose Bowl.)"

This was one of the two years there was such a thing as the Cherry Bowl in the Pontiac (Michigan) Silverdome. Poker-faced, Edwards inquired of Bo, "Isn't there a bowl in Detroit you could have gone to?"

That shut Bo up until someone asked how he could justify bringing a 6-5 team to play the No. 1-ranked team in the nation.

Bo harked back to the stretch between 1972-74 when Michigan never went to a bowl despite a 30-2-1 record and a couple of Big Ten championships. Because of the Big Ten's no-repeat rule, a ban on participation in all other bowls and one year a vote by conference athletic directors in favor of Ohio State, the Wolverines were shut out of post-season action. Bo allowed as how the Holiday Bowl made up for some of that.

YOU COULD NEEDLE BO BACK AND HE COULD TAKE IT AS WELL AS DISH IT OUT.

Knowing Bo as well as I did, I could get away with what I did next.

I went up to him and said, "You're lucky you didn't go to a bowl game in those three years."

He bit. "Why?" he asked.

"Because," I said, "your bowl record would be 2-12 instead of 2-9."

Bo muttered something which I didn't stick around long enough to hear. ✦

From Herschel Nissenson's book, Tales from College Football's Sidelines

Always prepared, Bo Schembechler reviews game film from the recliner in his office. *Tony Tomsic/Sports Illustrated*

"THEY CALL ME 'BO.' WE'RE ON A FIRST-NAME BASIS HERE."

—BO SCHEMBECHLER,
ON WHAT HIS PLAYERS CALL HIM

"WHEN YOUR TEAM IS WINNING, BE READY TO BE TOUGH, BECAUSE WINNING CAN MAKE YOU SOFT. ON THE OTHER HAND, WHEN YOUR TEAM IS LOSING, STICK BY THEM. KEEP BELIEVING."

—BO SCHEMBECHLER

BO'S WOLVERINE CAPTAINS

1969
Jim Mandich
1970
Don Moorhead, Henry Hill
1971
Frank Gusich, Guy Murdock
1972
Tom Coyle, Randy Logan
1973
Dave Gallagher, Paul Seal
1974
Dennis Franklin, David Brown
1975
Kirk Lewis, Don Dufek
1976
Rob Lytle, Calvin O'Neal, Kirk Lewis
1977
Dwight Hicks, Walt Downing
1978
Russell Davis, Jerry Meter
1979
John Arbeznik, Ron Simpkins
1980
Andy Cannavino, George Lilja
1981
Kurt Becker, Robert Thompson
1982
Anthony Carter, Paul Girgash, Robert Thompson
1983
Stefan Humphries, John Lott
1984
Doug James, Mike Mallory
1985
Brad Cochran, Eric Kattus, Mike Mallory
1986
Jim Harbaugh, Andy Moeller
1987
Jamie Morris, Doug Mallory
1988
Mark Messner, John Vitale
1989
J.J. Grant, Derrick Walker

There are a lot of stories that circulate about fiery pregame talks, or ranting and raving halftime speeches from coaches, that are sometimes blown out of proportion. Such is the case with Bo Schembechler's pregame talk to his team before the Ohio State game at Michigan Stadium in 1969.

The 24-12 Michigan win was one of the Wolverines' greatest triumphs over the No. 1-ranked and unbeaten Buckeyes. It came a year after Ohio State humbled Michigan 50-14 in Columbus. The rumors were that Bo played up the previous year's score and revved the team to such a fever pitch that we broke chairs and tore the door off the locker room before we headed down the tunnel to the field.

Here is the real story. I know. I was there.

During the week prior to the game, the scout team players wore white jerseys with scarlet numbers, like Ohio State's away jerseys. The jerseys also had the score 50-14 stenciled just below the throat on the front collar. The staff said nothing about the previous year's score. The reminder on the scout team jerseys was subtle, but the message was clear.

We had a great week of practice and were confident we could win, even though very few gave us any chance. In the locker room before the game there was a heightened sense of emotion, because we all knew this was huge. We were confident, not frightened.

When Bo addressed us prior to going out for the kickoff, he was serious and very much in control. He matter-of-factly looked at Henry Hill, our middle guard, and said, "Henry, is Jim Stillwagon [Ohio State's middle guard] better than you?" He then looked at Don Moorhead, our quarterback, and said, "Hey Moorhead, is Rex Kern [Ohio State's quarterback] better than you?"

Bo continued this line of questioning to about three or four more guys, asking if their Ohio State counterparts were better players. Of course the answer was an emphatic, "No!"

Bo had made his point. He didn't need to get loud to make it. At that point he raised his voice a little and said, "Men, if we play the way we are capable, if we don't turn the ball over, if we don't miss assignments, if we play hard and execute the fundamentals, we will win this game." After a moment of thoughtful silence, Bo shouted, "Now, let's go out and win!"

The idea that a pregame, rah-rah speech can make a difference was never a Schembechler characteristic. "If you want to motivate, to stimulate," Bo says, "it may come during the week. It may have come before you left the hotel to come to the locker room to dress. These speeches come from time to time when you think they are necessary."

Against Ohio State that November Saturday in 1969, it wasn't necessary. "There's no such thing as the ol' pregame/halftime, Let's Go Win One for the Gipper speech. At least not in my judgment," Bo concluded.

Based on what I know of that locker room before the 1969 Ohio State game, I believe Bo. He knew he didn't need to fire us up emotionally; we were already at an emotional peak. Bo wanted us to be focused on the job at hand. He was quiet but intense.

So remember, truth and fiction. The fiction makes a better story, but the truth is, Jim Mandich, our captain, did not rip the locker room door off its hinges. We didn't throw chairs against the walls, or break anything. All we did was win! ◆

From Herschel Nissenson's book, Tales from College Football's Sidelines

Bo Schembechler shouts instructions from the sideline during a game against Ohio State. *Tony Tomsic/Sports Illustrated*

Bo Schembechler
had two favorite expressions.

The first one was, *"That would have killed an ordinary man."* That's how he referred to almost every bad thing that happened to him. Once, in the early 1980s, one of his players knocked him down during a practice drill. Wide-eyed observers saw him eventually pop up and exclaim, "That would have killed an ordinary man."

His second catchphrase was a simple two-word question, *"Got it?"* When Bo spoke to his players or his staff members, he'd attach "Got it?" to his pointed statements. "I'm going to tell you something, got it?" he would say. "Pay attention, got it?"

Bo was a straight talker, and passed judgment on almost everything and everyone.

Michigan head coach Lloyd Carr (lower) was an assistant to the legendary Bo Schembechler (top) for 10 years (1980-89), before he was named head coach in 1995. *Albert Dickson/TSN/ZUMA Press/Icon SMI*

"WE HAVE LOST A GIANT AT MICHIGAN AND IN COLLEGE FOOTBALL. THERE WAS NEVER A GREATER AMBASSADOR FOR THE UNIVERSITY OF MICHIGAN, OR COLLEGE FOOTBALL, THAN BO. PERSONALLY, I HAVE LOST A MAN I LOVE."

—MICHIGAN COACH LLOYD CARR

"BO WAS A GIANT. HE WAS A GREAT FOOTBALL COACH AND PERSON. HE WAS A GREAT SUPPORTER OF COLLEGE FOOTBALL AND THE WAY IT'S SUPPOSED TO BE PLAYED. ... I'M NOT SURE HE HAS GOTTEN HIS DUE AS FAR AS BEING ONE OF THE TRULY GREAT FOOTBALL COACHES OF ALL-TIME. I'M GOING TO MISS HIM."

—PENN STATE COACH JOE PATERNO

BO: A TO Z

Bo served as Michigan's Athletic Director from 1988 to 1990

Big House has hosted 100,000+ fans for 200 consecutive games

Lloyd Carr, a former Schembechler assistant, now fills the Michigan head coaching position

Bo's Michigan teams led the Big Ten in Total Defense 11 times

As president of the Detroit Tigers in 1991, Bo fired Tigers radio broadcaster Ernie Harwell, a move decried by fans and the press

As U-M's A.D., Schembechler appointed Steve Fisher as Bill Frieder's replacement in March of 1989, and the U-M basketball team went on to win the NCAA championship

Glenn, Bo's given first name

Hail, Hail to Michigan

Integrity, no one had more than Bo

John "Jumbo" Elliott was perhaps Bo's greatest offensive lineman

Kicker Dana Coin's field goal vs. Ohio State helped send the undefeated 1971 Wolverines to the Rose Bowl

Rob Lytle, Bo's tailback in 1976, was the Big Ten's MVP that season

M, the block letter than he wore upon his ever-present baseball cap

Northwestern, the only Big Ten team that never beat Bo (0-14)

Schembechler was a native of Barberton, Ohio

Perfection: Bo's teams finished the Big Ten season with a perfect record three times

Quarterback Rick Leach was a three-time first-team All-Big Ten selection for Bo

Rose Bowl, the game in which Bo coached on 10 occasions

Sunglasses, a favorite Schembechler accessory

Tackle, Bo's position as a player at Miami of Ohio

Bob Ufer, The Voice of Michigan Football, was one of Bo's biggest boosters

Victories, of which Bo had 194 in 21 seasons at Michigan

Woody Hayes—Bo's mentor, bitter rival, and friend

After his first X (10) seasons, Bo had compiled seven seasons with ten-plus wins

Fielding Yost, the only Big Ten coach with a better winning percentage than Bo

Steve Zacharis was Bo's only letter winner whose last name started with the letter Z

Bo Schembechler has never been the type to spring surprises. So it was a pretty major surprise when Bo announced at the end of the 1989 season that he would retire as Michigan's coach after the Rose Bowl game on New Year's Day 1990. It was a surprise because Bo had just completed two of his most successful seasons. He had led Michigan to a pair of Big Ten championships in 1988 and 1989. The Wolverines had gone through those two years without a conference loss. The closest they came to losing was a tie at Illinois in 1988. Despite two heart bypass surgeries during his career at Michigan, Bo looked healthy and was coaching his best.

Bo knew it was over long before any of us did, though. After beating Ohio State 28-18 in 1989, he was interviewed on the field by ABC television. "Somebody said when ABC field reporter Mike Adamle interviewed me after that game," Bo recalls, "that I didn't even smile. Probably the reason for that was I realized then, that I had just coached my last game in Michigan Stadium."

It wasn't until a couple of weeks later that Bo let everybody know at a press conference that he was through. "I'm sad at leaving," Bo told the gathered press. "I hate to leave the players. I hate to leave coaching, but it's time to go."

Just like he was during his career, Bo was direct and to the point. It was a no-nonsense announcement. In retrospect, Bo knew it was the right thing to do for himself and his family. But as you might expect, he didn't go without a fight. "Since the second heart operation, my doctors had been after me to slow down," Bo laughs. "They kept telling me I just couldn't keep going like this. I was 60 years old, and they told me I couldn't keep pushing myself. The doctors told me they didn't feel that I could ever just step back to a lesser role because I was too conscientious. They told me the only way I could do it was to divorce myself from the athletic program.

"With all that weighing on me, I knew I had to go," Bo says matter-of-factly. "And when I made the decision to retire, I never looked back, and I still don't. It was the right thing to do. It was the right

A full Michigan Stadium was a sight to which Bo Schembechler soon became accustomed. Scott Boehm/Getty Images

time to do it," Bo says with great pride. "It was the job I loved the most. I'll never have a job like the one I left. It was the most gratifying job that I'll ever have. But I walked away and the program was intact. It was not in disarray. I was not chased out of town. There were no violations of recruiting rules that forced me to resign. And all of the great people that contributed over my 21 years were still with me, and that is unheard of in intercollegiate athletics. To be able to do that made me very, very proud."

Schembechler may have stopped coaching Michigan, but he never left Michigan football. The issue was not that he didn't want to coach anymore; rather, it was that he couldn't coach the only way he knew how. "In my prime, I could coach any position, anywhere, anyhow," Bo says with conviction. "I could study film for eight hours a day and never stop. I could do all those things, but it was coming to the point where maybe I couldn't do it anymore. I didn't want to go on and on and on, to where the job became a burden. I didn't want it to become too hard for me to do. If I couldn't be the guy that I was before, and I couldn't coach all-out, then let's get somebody else in here that could."

Bo has never been the kind of person to hype himself. He has never said that he's anything more than a football coach. He staunchly defends his for-

mer occupation as an honorable profession. He is modest and spreads the credit around. Even as he stepped down as coach, he deflected the credit. "It could have been somebody else that got the Michigan job in 1969," Bo says, "and probably done the same things that I've done, maybe even better."

There are many who would argue with Bo about that, including yours truly. He is a remarkable man, and his accomplishments at Michigan are legendary. Hundreds of young men are better off today than when they enrolled at Michigan because of their association with Bo. There is one thing he unashamedly admits that he did bring with him when he accepted the job at Michigan that Bo feels nobody else would have, "If anybody else would have taken this job, there is one thing I know for sure. They wouldn't have had the respect for the job like I had. It was the best thing that ever happened to me in my life." ✦

From Jim Brandstatter's book, Tales from Michigan Stadium

Tony Tomsic/Sports Illustrated

Paul Jasienski/Getty Images

BO'S MICHIGAN RECORD

Year	Overall	Big Ten (finish)
1969	8-3-0	6-1-0 (T-1st)
1970	9-1-0	6-1-0 (T-2nd)
1971	11-1-0	8-0-0 (1st)
1972	10-1-0	7-1-0 (T-1st)
1973	10-0-1	7-0-1 (T-1st)
1974	10-1-0	7-1-0 (T-1st
1975	8-2-2	7-1-0 (2nd)
1976	10-2-0	7-1-0 (T-1st)
1977	10-2-0	7-1-0 (T-1st)
1978	10-2-0	7-1-0 (T-1st)
1979	8-4-0	6-2-0 (3rd)
1980	10-2-0	8-0-0 (1st)
1981	9-3-0	6-3-0 (T-3rd)
1982	8-4-0	8-1-0 (1st)
1983	9-3-0	8-1-0 (2nd)
1984	6-6-0	5-4-0 (T-6th)
1985	10-1-1	6-1-1 (2nd)
1986	11-2-0	7-1-0 (T-1st)
1987	8-4-0	5-3-0 (4th)
1988	9-2-1	7-0-1 (1st)
1989	10-2-0	8-0-0 (1st)
Total	**194-48-5**	**143-24-3**

"THE HALLMARK OF ANY GREAT FOOTBALL PROGRAM IS COMPLETE HONESTY BETWEEN THE COACHES AND THE PLAYERS. THERE'S GOT TO BE A TRUST BETWEEN THE TWO. AND BO WAS ALWAYS, ALWAYS HONEST AND SO SINCERE."

—FORMER WEST VIRGINIA COACH DON NEHLEN

"THE STATE OF OHIO AND THE STATE OF MICHIGAN HAS LOST A GREAT MAN, HAS LOST A GREAT COACH, AND A GREAT DAD. IN MY OPINION, BO SCHEMBECHLER IS THE GREATEST FOOTBALL COACH MICHIGAN EVER HAD."

—FORMER OHIO STATE COACH EARLE BRUCE

COACHES ON BO

"HE USED TO CALL ME 'DOOLEY OF GEORGIA' IN HIS TOUGH YANKEE ACCENT, AND I WOULD CALL HIM 'SCHEMBECHLER OF MICHIGAN' WITH MY SOUTHERN DRAWL. HE PERSON-ALLY GAVE THAT TOUGH OUTWARD APPEARANCE, BUT HE HAD A SOFT SPIRIT AND A GREAT SENSE OF HUMOR."

—FORMER GEORGIA COACH VINCE DOOLEY

"BO SCHEMBECHLER EPITOMIZED BIG TEN FOOT-BALL. ...HE PRODUCED FUNDAMENTALLY SOUND, HARD-NOSED TEAMS. HIS TEAMS PLAYED FOOTBALL THE WAY THE GAME IS SUPPOSED TO BE PLAYED."

—FORMER WISCONSIN COACH BARRY ALVAREZ

BO'S ALL-BIG TEN
DEFENSIVE PLAYERS

Tom Curtis, DB, 1969
Marty Huff, LB, 1969-70
Henry Hill, MG, 1970
Thom Darden, DB, 1970-71
Mike Taylor, LB, 1971
Clint Spearman, DE, 1972
Fred Grambau, DT, 1972
Randy Logan, DB, 1972
Dave Brown, DB, 1972-73-74
Dave Gallagher, DT, 1973
Steve Strinko, LB, 1974
Dan Jilek, DE, 1974-75
Jeff Perlinger, DT, 1974
Tim Davis, MG, 1974-75
Don Dufek, DB, 1974-75
Greg Morton, DT, 1975-76
Calvin O'Neal, LB, 1975-76
John Anderson, LB, 1976-77
Dwight Hicks, DB, 1977
Jim Pickens, DB, 1977
Curtis Greer, DT, 1978-79
Ron Simpkins, LB, 1978-79
Mike Jolly, DB, 1978-79
Mike Harden, DB, 1978
Mike Trgovac, MG, 1979-80
Mel Owens, LB, 1980
Andy Cannavino, LB, 1980
Robert Thompson, LB, 1982
Paul Girgash, LB, 1982
Keith Bostic, DB, 1982
Kevin Brooks, DT, 1983-84
Al Sincich, MG, 1983
Evan Cooper, DB, 1983
Mike Mallory, LB, 1984-85
Brad Cochran, DB, 1985
Mike Hammerstein, DT, 1985
Mark Messner, DT, 1985-86-87-88
Andy Moeller, LB, 1986
Garland Rivers, DB, 1986
David Arnold, DB, 1988
Tripp Welborne, DB, 1989

BO'S ALL-BIG TEN
RUNNING BACKS

Billy Taylor, 1969-70
Ed Shuttlesworth, 1972-73
Gordon Bell, 1975
Rob Lytle, 1976
Russell Davis, 1978
Butch Woolfolk, 1979-81
Lawrence Ricks, 1982
Jamie Morris, RB, 1986-87
Tony Boles, 1988-89

BO'S ALL-BIG TEN
QUARTERBACKS

Don Moorhead, 1970
Dennis Franklin, 1973
Rick Leach, 1976-77-78
Jim Harbaugh, 1986

Bo Schembechler lets loose with one of his famous sideline tirades during the 1986 Ohio State matchup.
Tony Tomsic/Sports Illustrated

WOLVERINES HONOR BO WITH EFFORT

By Jim Litke, Associated Press
November. 18, 2006

Bo knows. Even in defeat, there was no better way this Michigan squad could have honored Bo Schembechler's memory and proved it learned his lessons than the way it fought back time after time against Ohio State.

The stubbornness the Wolverines displayed by run, run, running themselves back into the game in the second half; the way they didn't quit until the clock made them; the fierceness they showed skeptics who said a rematch in the national title game wouldn't be the best outcome to this madcap season—those were all things that the old man would have loved.

For all that, Lloyd Carr wanted to be sure everyone knew that his mentor's death a day earlier had nothing to do with the outcome of The Game.

"I want to be clear," Carr began his postgame news conference, choking back tears after the Buckeyes claimed a 42-39 win over the Wolverines for an automatic berth in the national title game. "It would not be fair to Bo.

"I'm a little mad at him because he didn't stay around for this game. But it wouldn't be fair to use that in any way, and we don't. And all I could say about him," Carr paused, his voice cracking one more time, "is I loved that man."

Everybody who ever looked in on this most storied of rivalries feels that way.

Schembechler and his mentor, Ohio State legend Woody Hayes, turned it into the best game on the college football calendar most every year, something even the kids who were born after both coaches were gone from the sideline knew. Just before kickoff, one of them hoisted a sign that read, "Bo and Woody in Heaven: Play Nice."

A Michigan fan remembers Bo Schembechler in the stands on Saturday, November 18, 2006, during the game between top-rated Ohio State and No. 2 Michigan in Columbus. AP/WWP

Ohio State coach Jim Tressel (right) talks with Michigan coach Lloyd Carr before the start of their game on November 18, 2006. Gregory Shamus/Getty Images

Mike Hart recalled. "That's Bo—offensive and defensive lines win games."

But while he didn't get the specifics right during his talk, Schembechler's example—even in death—steeled the Wolverines for what was to come.

"It's sad to see him go," said quarterback Chad Henne, who like Hart posted very respectable numbers in his third consecutive loss to the Buckeyes.

But the first thing Henne thought about when the news of Schembechler's death just a few minutes before noon Friday was this: "You've got to take advantage of every opportunity you've got, because he was there one day, and then he's gone the next.

"We dearly miss him," he added. "We tried to fight for him today."

None of the Wolverines, though, missed him more than Carr.

Schembechler hired him in 1980 to coach his secondary and taught him the Michigan way of doing things. That involved everything from bringing in music students to tutor the players on singing "The Victors" to teaching his lineman blocking schemes that were every bit as intricate as a ballroom waltz.

Trying to honor those lessons, Carr steeled himself from the second the news arrived to the bitter end of Saturday's classic. He asked his kids not to use Bo as motivation—or even worse, an excuse. He asked only that each of them "coach and play in a way that would honor him."

And good as his word, Carr refused to lobby his colleagues, anybody else who votes in the polls, or even the public for a rematch. Afterward, he conceded that telling his kids of Schembechler's death "was hard and it was emotional, yet all of us have challenges and you've got to move on.

Back on the slippery turf of Ohio Stadium, though, their successors played it any way but that. What was supposed to be a tractor pull between two of the country's toughest defenses played out like the 24 Hours of Daytona instead—an endurance race in which the Buckeyes zoomed out ahead with one big play after another, yet still struggled to get Michigan out of its rearview mirror.

Not surprisingly, Schembechler anticipated just the opposite when he talked to the team Thursday.

"He just said if we want to win, we've got to come out and win the line of scrimmage," running back

"You've got to deal," he said, "with whatever comes your way."

Carr did that as capably as he could, wiping a tear when he climbed on the bus Friday afternoon in Ann Arbor and then going about his business the last 24 hours with a resolve that would have made Schembechler proud.

"He wasn't, you know, emotional," defensive end LaMarr Woodley said. "He wasn't really showing it because he didn't want to bring any guys on the team down. We feed off our coach, so he was just trying to stay positive."

That was never tougher than on Saturday, knowing that he likely lost a shot at the national title, that he lost to Ohio State archrival Jim Tressel for the fifth time in six games, and can't even be certain whether the Rose Bowl will hold open a slot for his Wolverines.

After all they'd gone through and given up, somebody asked Carr how tough it would be waiting to find out where his team, arguably still the second best in the nation, would be playing next. For the first time, maybe, all afternoon, his reddened eyes lit up and his lips grudgingly parted in a smile.

"I have no idea," he said. "I guess we'll find out."

Wherever that turns out to be, Carr can count on this much: Bo will be looking on. ✦

Mourners pay their respects to Bo Schembechler during a public viewing at St. Andrews Episcopal Church in Ann Arbor, on Sunday, November 19, 2006. AP/WWP

Celebrate Michigan sports in these other great books from Sports Publishing!

Michigan: Where Have You Gone?
by Jim Cnockaert

- 6 x 9 hardcover
- 256 pages
- photos throughout
- $24.95

Tales from the Detroit Tigers Dugout
by Jack Ebling

- 5.5 x 8.25 hardcover
- 192 pages
- photos throughout
- $19.95 (Coming Spring 2007)

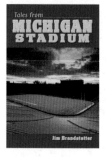

Tales from Michigan Stadium
by Jim Brandstatter

- 5.5 x 8.25 softcover
- 192 pages
- photos throughout
- $14.95

Tales from Michigan Stadium: Volume II
by Jim Brandstatter

- 5.5 x 8.25 hardcover
- 192 pages
- photos throughout
- $19.95

Charlie Sanders's Tales from the Detroit Lions
by Charlie Sanders with Larry Paladino

- 5.5 x 8.25 softcover
- 192 pages
- photos throughout
- $19.95

Centered by a Miracle: A True Story of Friendship, Football, and Life
by Steve Rom and Rod Payne

- 6 x 9 hardcover
- 256 pages
- photos throughout
- $24.95 (2006 release)

Detroit Pistons: Champions at Work
by The Detroit News

- 8.5 x 11 hard/softcover
- 128 pages • color photos throughout
- $19.95 (hardcover)
- $14.95 (softcover)

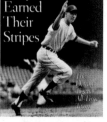

They Earned Their Stripes: The Detroit Tigers' All-Time Team
by The Detroit News

- 8.5 x 11 hard/softcover
- 192 pages
- photos throughout
- $29.95 (hardcover)
- $17.95 (softcover)

Great Detroit Sports Debate
by Drew Sharp and Terry Foster

- 6 x 9 softcover
- 256 pages
- $16.95

Tales from the Detroit Pistons
by Perry A. Farrell with Reflections from Rick Mahorn and Joe Dumars

- 5.5 x 8.25 hardcover
- 192 pages
- photos throughout
- $19.95